COL Thomas Guthrie

LIFE
LESSONS AND
LEADERSHIP
TIPS

outskirtspress
DENVER, COLORADO

These are the ramblings (very organized ramblings, as per my somewhat anal retentive nature) of a guy who has been leading people and soldiers since I was a six-year-old shortstop for the Waynewood Village No Names (we were the only team not to have a sponsor, so we just wore green T-shirts…we won the league championship).

Let's Go

I am a US Army infantryman. I know of nothing more satisfying. It is an honor to serve with such men. Maybe only policemen/firemen have a similar bond: that of relying on your buddies to keep the group alive. Unlike many officers, who may have grown into the Army over time, I pretty much knew that I wanted to be an Airborne Ranger Infantry Officer from about the time I was 15 years old. Dad, a retired Army Officer himself, really had nothing to do with that decision other than providing me a superb example of what it was to be a man, a husband and a father.

I cannot leave out the women in my life. My seemingly quiet mother was actually the one in control of the family environment. Dad might smack us once in a while, but the most devastating thing I could ever hear was when Mom said, "Tom, I am disappointed that you did that".

My beautiful, smart, fit, and loving wife keeps me grounded. "Hey, Defender of the Free World, the trash needs to go out, the dog has not been walked and you have to help your daughter with some 9th grade math homework". Perfect. I "married up" as they say.

Before we get started, a little sage advice that Pop gave me the day I was commissioned as a 2LT of Infantry: *"Treat every job you have as if it is the most important one that you will ever have, and everything else will work out just fine."* Great advice for anyone, anywhere, in any occupation. He also told me, *"There is no such thing as a personality conflict with your boss."* Another great life lesson.

Since the majority of folks who might actually read this are in the military, I know that time is of the essence. I survived college off of Cliff notes, so I will do everyone a favor: I will give you the entire "book" in the first few pages. If you decide to read further, then fine. These comments have been scribed over the course of over 27 years of military service (which seems like it has gone way too fast). I started keeping a record of "lessons and tips" when I was a 1LT because I realized that my perceptions would most likely change over time and I did not want to lose sight of the "facts" as I perceived them at that point in time. It is important to acknowledge that time does have a way of clouding your memory. A 48-year-old man "forgets" that he used to blare his stereo with "God awful" music and that driving fast, although illegal, was still pretty cool as long as you didn't get caught and even more cool if there was a pretty girl in the car with you.

What follows are my Life Lessons and Leadership Tips. Few of these are original thoughts, but then again most good ideas have already been thought of by someone else, and I hate wasting time. Where I know or remember the originator, I will give him his due.

Life Lessons and Leadership Tips

1. The Army is my life, but it isn't my **whole** life. Lots of folks preach "balance," but don't demonstrate it themselves. That's hypocritical. Soldiers and junior leaders will believe only what they see in this area. Be the example.
2. Teach, train, validate, and assign responsibility, then trust those below you. Underwrite mistakes made in the effort to better the organization. Your subordinates will repay you in kind. In the process you will have trained the next generation of leaders to think and execute.
3. 99% of soldiers want to do the right thing. 1% do not. Remove the 1% using the least amount of organizational energy possible.
4. Work fast, stay focused, and save most of the "war-story telling" for later and you will get home for dinner with your family. In the process you will have actually done more for the organization as well.
5. Ask yourself:
   a. Do you really need this meeting that is scheduled?
   b. If yes, then who really needs to be there?
   c. If more people are attending than are really needed tell them not to come. They can go get something productive done.

6. Do you love soldiers enough to stay in the Army long enough to actually affect change and improve the institution?

7. When time is tight and you know you are right, remember, "We protect democracy, we don't always have to practice it" (attributed to then-LTC Paul L).

8. You will get better results if you talk **to and with** soldiers and leaders instead of talking **at** them. There is a huge difference.

9. Compete against yourself and your own expectations of your unit. Don't worry about what the Jones' are doing.

10. Remember your friends along the way. There will be some who aren't moving as "fast" as you. Don't push them aside. Some will move faster than you. Don't be envious or jealous. In the end, most of us get what we earn.

11. "Hooah, Sir" has about 20 different meanings. You better know them all, or you'll think everyone is happy and motivated all of the time.

12. No matter how "high" you rise, do not forget that most troops find the following things most important — and the order in which they are prioritized changes depending on many factors: The Opposite Sex, Beer, **Good training, Time off, Food**. You (the leader) can affect **three** of the five.

13. The 10-70-20 rule. A theory for getting things done in an organized way. When given a complex task or mission, the leader must spend the first 10% of the overall time determining the best, most efficient way in which it should be accomplished (sets the framework, guidance, and directives required). 70% of the effort/work is done by others (delegate). In the Army this is called the "nug"

work. The last 20% is the leader supervising the effort and keeping them on track.

14. Physical conditioning is and always has been the great equalizer. Even if you are in the process of getting yelled at, there is great solace in knowing that you could "choke the guy out" if you had to. Being in good shape breeds confidence.

15. When **ambition** becomes ***expectation***, the boundary between confidence and arrogance has just been crossed. Ambition is good. I have ambition. If I start *expecting* the Army to give me things (promotions, command, choice of assignment, etc), then I just went too far. We serve the Army more than the Army serves us.

16. Do not determine your self-worth solely based on your proximity to the target (attributed to MG G, former JSOC Commander).

17. Tactics. When has anyone "loved" the Operations Order of their higher headquarters? The answer is hardly ever. Remember that you are someone else's higher headquarters too.

18. The term "Leader Flexibility," briefed at routine Training Meetings as a unit strength, is a synonym for "we can't plan anything, but folks are good at jumping through their butt at the last minute." Flexibility and adaptability are desired traits for leaders, but training management systems should be relatively inflexible if true predictability is to occur.

19. "It is easy to march to the sound of the guns when you are at the head of the column" (attributed to then-LTC Mike K). How you perform and act in supporting roles reveals your true nature and that of your unit.

20. Discipline is the constantly repeated act of correct choice (a quote from a female bodybuilder in one of those muscle-head magazines).
21. Make regular and personal contact with your counterparts (peers) on your right and left. Not doing so regularly breeds an exclusionary climate and, over time, a feeling of isolation within the larger organization.
22. As a leader, never have your entire calendar "filled."
23. Leading Organizations. It is not so much what you do or how much you accomplish, but what you do/accomplish with what you have to work with. How high the bar (the standard) is raised is in direct correlation to the unit's, or individual's, potential.
24. "Badges and resumes" impress most soldiers and junior officers initially, and in many circles afford the opportunity to at least get your foot in the door. That honeymoon lasts about two days.
25. "The function of leadership is to produce more leaders, not more followers" (I think Ralph Nader said this).
26. Strive to never be the "**But** Man."
27. If there is a major problem in your unit start looking for the cause of it by applying ever widening concentric circles around your desk.
28. "Nothing is impossible for a man who does not have to execute it" (then-LTC Joe V, circa 1996).
29. Be mindful and wary of the leader who artfully changes the use of pronouns depending on the circumstances.
30. Be polite, be courteous, but have a plan to crush everyone you meet just in case.
31. At the end of the day (meaning your career), all that will be remembered about you is: (a) how you treated people and (b) your reputation.

32. Avoid the inevitable temptation to define the quality of your service by the rank, title, and position held at the end of that service.

꒰꒰꒱

The Army is my life, but it isn't my whole life. Lots of folks preach "balance," but don't demonstrate it themselves. That's hypocritical. Soldiers and junior leaders will believe only what they see in this area. Be the example.

"Balance" is probably the most misused word in the Army vernacular. Senior officers (MAJs on up) often preach it, but few actually do it. They work weekends as badges of honor and will think that since they attended little Susie's recital on Thursday night it covers them for "family time" this week. Balance, to me, is doing the job at hand and doing it well, while simultaneously really taking care of your family. If the only time you come home is when your wife calls to remind you to be somewhere for her or your kids, then you have no balance. The family, in this case, is relegated to an entry in your "To Do" list.

Bill Cosby interviewed about 100 kids and asked them the question, "What are Dads for?" The generalized answer was, "**Dads are just to be with**." Military dads often equate being a good husband and father with "doing things"…we call it "quality time." What the family really needs is simply your presence, whether you are doing something or not.

By the way, single soldiers and officers are allowed to have lives too.

Teach, train, validate, and assign responsibility, then trust those below you. Underwrite mistakes made in the effort to better the organization. Your subordinates will repay you in kind. In the process you will have trained the next generation of leaders to think and execute.

Nobody starts off knowing everything. There is, and always will be, some discovery learning required when someone starts a new job. Self-study, On the Job Training (OJT), and "baptism by fire," are all worthy ways to learn and should be retained, but in most cases the supervisor must first **teach** the subordinate what it is he is supposed to do. Within a short period of time (hopefully), the supervisor then validates the work and competence of the subordinate. Once validated the subordinate is then expected to perform (gets responsibility assigned). Depending on the subordinate's capabilities, the superior can then step back and focus on other priorities because he has earned trust. Too often in the military we skip the first couple of steps and go directly to assigning responsibility. Accept high risk and failures when this is the norm.

**99% of soldiers want to do the right thing.
1% do not. Remove the 1% using the least amount of
organizational energy possible.**

Many leaders get frustrated over the 1%. They take up time and energy and there are always mountains of paperwork associated with them. When writing this tip back in 2002 I commanded about 700 soldiers and, on any given day, there were 10 or so that were in "trouble." If I had a negative outlook on life then it would be easy for me to focus all my attention on these problem soldiers and become consumed worrying about some perceived "organizational or leadership failure." Slap yourself if this happening to you. There are 690 soldiers who are doing all they can and they need your positive leadership focused on them. Rehabilitate soldiers where you can, but don't lose sleep if the facts lead you to separate a soldier from the Army.

༄༄༄

**Work fast, stay focused, and save most of the
"war-story telling" for later and you will get home for
dinner with your family. In the process you will have
actually done more for the organization as well.**

Other than the soldiers themselves, which are our most precious resource, time is what everybody wants more of and normally cannot have. Have you ever been in an organization where all the meetings start 15 minutes late? If you have just four meetings a week, then you just had an hour stolen from you. I can get a lot done in an hour; how about you? Have you ever been in unit where the weekly, 60-minute meeting habitually takes 90 minutes? All these occurrences are time thieves.

My goal has always been to get home for dinner and yes, it has been achievable and yes, I have had all the jobs where people said, "You'll never see your family in that job..." and no, I did not go back to work after dinner.

Let's talk about self-inflicted time thievery. Some Army leaders come into work just minutes before they have to (6:30 a.m. formation). After physical training they go home to shower and change and maybe have breakfast. They go back into work about 9:00 then they take off for lunch at 11:30. They come back at 1:00 p.m. and work. During the afternoon they run into a buddy and they talk about "stuff" for 30 minutes. The leader wonders why he hasn't gotten much done today and resigns himself to having to work late tonight. He calls his wife to let her know. She is not surprised.

During the majority of my career I woke up around 4:45 a.m. and was in the office no later than 5:15 to get about 60-75 minutes of uninterrupted work done before first formation. After physical training (PT), I showered at the office and was back to working around 8:00. I ate in the mess hall for lunch instead of going home and was back at work 30-40 minutes later. I was out the door and headed home by 5:30 p.m. Who got the most out of the day?

My wife and kids are asleep whether I wake up at 0600, or 0445. Either way, they aren't missing me in the morning. On the other hand they would miss me if I didn't get home until 7:30 p.m. Programming my days like this I am home to eat dinner, help with homework, give baths, pick them up from practice, etc. I am not asking for you to vote me for Father of the Year (far from it) but if you miss this stuff, then you are missing out on life. Don't miss this huge part of life by your own doings. You will be deployed for training, or for real, and won't be around at all during those times. Why would you choose to be a "ghost" to your family when you do have the time?

Ask yourself:
a. Do you really need this meeting that is scheduled?
b. If yes, then who really needs to be there?
c. If more people are attending than are really needed tell them not to come. They can go get something productive done.

Meetings are inevitable, but the Army can sometimes take it to a whole new level. I only like meetings that result in decisions and/or directives. As a commander, information-sharing meetings don't do a whole lot for me. If I need information then either I'll ask for it or if a subordinate knows that I need to know the information then he'll send it to me.

When the "boss" shows up for a meeting, guess what? All kinds of people show up…even if they don't really need to be there. They show up even when they have nothing of value to add to the meeting. Why? Ship them off to go do something productive. Whenever I have a meeting I look around the room and see who really needs to be there. If they are not needed I send them away. You'd be amazed at how many man-hours are literally wasted because their attendance becomes "mandatory or expected" over time. It becomes habit: a bad habit.

I avoid meetings whenever possible. It frees up "wandering around time" and that is where I can get a lot of good information. Not "Gotcha!" information, as some leaders are prone to do, but information as seen through the eyes of the troops, or through other leaders who may not have a direct line to you often. Remember to temper this information as well, since it is truly from their perspective and not necessarily a well rounded, completely informed one.

If you are in charge, start and end meetings on time, exactly. Don't be late for anyone. 10:00 a.m. means 10:00 a.m., not 10:07 a.m. If you get pulled away to do something of higher priority or are running late because of something out of your control then let your next level subordinate handle the original meeting for you. Don't stop the train and in the process upset everyone else's schedule, just because you could not be there. You can only appreciate the "ripple effect" when you are the guy at the end of the ripple.

Do you love soldiers enough to stay in the Army long enough to actually affect change and improve the institution?

Pretty self-explanatory, so I will not spend much time on this one. You can gripe all you want, but the mark of a leader is to affect change, solve problems, and provide direction. You can't do that if you are not in the game.

꒱꒱꒱

When time is tight and you know you are right,
remember,
"We protect democracy; we don't always have to
practice it."

It's nice to have a consensus but in any large organization it is rarely achievable. Don't delay a decision when it is needed, but definitely don't delay the unpopular ones. Explain why you decided what you did, then move on. Not everybody has to like it. You are in charge for a reason.

꒱꒱꒱

You will get better results if you talk **to and with**
soldiers and leaders instead of talking **at** them.
There is a huge difference.

I think this is my favorite tip and I say it often. It comes naturally to some, but not to others. Soldiers have something to offer and too often we (officers) seem to believe that they are just good for doing what we tell them. Wrong. I had a training room clerk (Specialist, E-4) who had a master's degree in physics and was a published aerospace author. I have known Staff Sergeants (SSG) who have accumulated a net worth of over a million dollars through investments. You will never find out this kind of stuff if you sequester yourself in your office or meet everyone on your terms. There is great energy in a commander/leader who talks with soldiers, and not just for the purposes of finding out the dirt of a subordinate element.

Never be too busy to talk with a subordinate. GEN Patton said, "No good decision was ever made in a swivel chair." Good advice.

ﾉﾉﾉﾉ

Compete against yourself and your own expectations of your unit. Don't worry about what the Jones' are doing.

Every Mom and Dad in America has said the following at one time or another. It goes like this, "Would you jump off a bridge, if Johnny did?" I borrow good ideas and programs from others but only implement them if it fits my organization. Every unit is different so do not feel compelled to copy another unit's idea just because they did something that was viewed as good by others. Additionally, just because a good idea (one you had) worked well in your last unit, that doesn't mean it is appropriate or will work in your current one.

ﾉﾉﾉﾉ

Remember your friends along the way. There will be some who aren't moving as "fast" as you. Don't push them aside. Some will move faster than you. Don't be envious or jealous. In the end, most of us get what we earned.

I read a pretty cool book titled, "The Paradoxical Ten Commandments" and one of the commandments said, "If you are successful, then you will win false friends and true ene-mies...*Succeed anyway.*" Some guys are very good. Some, like me, got lucky (right places, right timing, right bosses, etc). Some are very good *and* lucky. A similarly talented leader may not reap the same benefits. That does not mean he is any less competent or qualified. Getting over that (not being picked for something or not being lucky) and being satisfied with the contribution you are making is hugely impressive.

"Hooah, Sir" has about 20 different meanings. You better know them all, or you'll think everyone is happy and motivated all of the time.

One of my favorites. In the civilian sector the equivalent is your boss asking you, "How's it going?" and the automatic response is something like, "Great, Sir," even though you just lost the largest account in the firm, your wife just left you and your dog got hit by the garbage truck this morning. Leaders who are visible and approachable to the people they lead stand a better chance of finding out the real truth than those who are not. An Army saying goes like this, "When the troops stop bringing you their problems, that's when you are in trouble." Open communication is a must. **Dialogue** is a two-way conversation. If just one person (the leader) talks all the time, then that's a **monologue** with people usually nodding in silent, if not indifferent, agreement. A Captain will not willingly set up an office call with a Colonel in order to unload his problems but he might talk about them if the Colonel sits next to him at lunch unexpectedly.

No matter how "high" you rise, do not forget that most troops find the following things most important — and the order in which they are prioritized changes depending on many factors: The Opposite Sex, Beer, **Good training, Time off, Food.** You can affect **three** of the five.

This was the first lesson I ever wrote. I was a 23-year-old 1LT. Being a LT is the most unique leadership experience you can ever have. You are much younger than most of your immediate subordinates and generally the same age as the majority of the "Joes," yet you are expected to lead and train them and set the example for them: Awesome. As you get older you forget what it was like to be young and bulletproof. It's kind of like being a father with teenage sons. Dad is always on you for "stupid" things like coming home on time, picking up after yourself, completing your chores to some mythical standard, etc. Now that I am a Dad, those things really **are** important. I wrote this one so that no matter how old I get I won't forget the mindset of a young man, especially that of a young soldier.

〜〜〜

The 10-70-20 rule. A theory for getting things done in an organized way. When given a complex task or mission, the leader must spend the first 10% of the overall time determining the best, most efficient way in which it should be accomplished (sets the framework, milestones, guidance, and directives required). 70% of the effort/work is done by others (delegate). In the Army this is called the "nug" work.

The last 20% is the leader supervising the effort and keeping them on track.

This tip addresses organizational effectiveness and the leader's role in it. Simply handing out tasks to subordinates is easy, but rarely is it effective in the long run. The leader's job is to give the subordinates not only the task (the what), but also the intent/purpose of the task (the **why**, which is vastly more important). Depending on the complexity of the task and its relative importance the leader often has to set the framework (some of the "how to") for the subordinate, so that time and energy is not wasted.

If, as a leader, you find yourself doing much more than the up-front 10% or the back-end 20% then look around. There are probably a few subordinates who are not earning their paychecks. As long as you do their job for them, they will let you.

❧❧❧

Physical conditioning is and always has been the great equalizer. Even if you are in the process of getting yelled at, there is great solace in knowing that you could "choke the guy out" if you had to. Being in good shape breeds confidence.

If you can't take the occasional ass-chewing then the Army (and probably business) is not for you. I have had mine chewed by some of the world's finest, but always tried to remain calm because I knew that it was the result of a specific, professional failing and in no way meant to demean me personally. I recall, as 1LT, getting chewed out so well by a Battalion Executive Officer, a MAJ, that I had a near, out of body experience. Right in the middle of his yelling I stopped listening completely (Zen strategy) and was in silent admiration of the quality of the ass-chewing that I was the receiving. I wanted to compliment him on his volume, passion, and most notably, his limited vocabulary. I, of course, just saluted and left the area very quickly.

꒰꒱꒰꒱

> When **ambition** becomes *expectation*, the boundary between confidence and arrogance has just been crossed. Ambition is good. I have ambition. If I start *expecting* the Army to give me things (promotions, command, choice of assignment, etc), then I just went too far. We serve the Army more than the Army serves us.

Somewhere during the course of my career I noticed a subtle shift in Army philosophy. It appears to me that personal preference has become a perceived **right,** not just a factor in determining where we will serve and what we will do. We used to just salute and move out when given a new job or a new posting. It is apparent that the Army is trying to care more about *what the individual leader wants to do*, sometimes to the detriment of the needs of the Army. Interesting shift. This could begin to foster an attitude of "selfish," not selfless, service. An officer who doesn't get his first choice (of job or of assignment) now believes that he is getting "screwed." In the end, the Army must put you where they need you and if it happens to be in a job and/or location that you like, then great.

It is not *the* over-riding factor, however, and we should not expect it to be.

"Do not determine your self-worth solely based on your proximity to the target".

Since I command infantrymen, I need them to believe that they are the biggest, baddest things walking the planet. Given the training, the elements, heavy exertion, and mental toughness that they have to endure and display daily, I would want nothing less. In fact, I go out of my way to tell them things like, "Men, the infantryman is the most genetically superior being in the world"...stuff like that. Having said that, it doesn't mean that I have to ridicule or demean some other soldier just because he/she isn't an infantryman. This is a volunteer Army and as much as I would personally never want to be an 88M (truck driver) I do not begrudge that soldier from wanting to be one. I do, however, expect that he/she be the best truck driver they can be, just like I expect the soldiers that I have commanded to be their best. There will always be competition between front-line soldiers and those "in the rear." Evaluate soldiers based on their job performance, not their title. I want a truck driver to be a very good truck driver. I don't expect him to be a very good machine gunner.

Tactics. When has anyone "loved" the Operations Order of their higher headquarters? Answer is hardly ever. Remember that you are someone else's higher headquarters too.

The easiest thing to do in any large organization is blame all the bad things that happen on the next higher level of authority. If I thought for one minute that the members of my current higher headquarters wake up in the morning thinking, "How can I screw Guthrie's unit today?" then I would truly be in need of some special care…the kind where the walls are rubber and you drink food through a straw.

༄༄༄

The term "Leader Flexibility," briefed at routine Training Meetings as a unit strength is a synonym for "We can't plan anything, but folks are good at jumping through their butt at the last minute." Flexibility and adaptability are desired traits for leaders in combat, but training management systems should be relatively inflexible if true predictability is to occur.

A completely military-oriented lesson with almost no parallel in the civilian sector that I know of. I could write a book on this tenant alone, but no one would want to read it. I'll move along.

༄༄༄

It is easy to "march to the sound of the guns when you are at the head of the column". How you perform and act in supporting roles reveals your true nature and that of your unit.

How true. When the focus of attention is on you, or your unit (the Army calls it the decisive or main effort), it's pretty easy to accomplish the task. The majority of resources and support are given to you, so you cannot help but be successful. Since you happen to be the primary focus at that point in time, there are others of equal position/status (your peers) that are not. A true team player will still do his best in those supporting roles. It's funny to watch a leader try and make his supporting effort appear as if it is really the decisive effort. I call this "Fear of Subordination." It's almost as if the leader can't stand the fact that he is not in the spotlight. This is childish behavior at best and certainly counter-productive to the larger organization's goals and objectives. There would be no linemen in football if everyone thought this way, only quarterbacks.

Discipline is the constantly repeated act of correct choice (a quote from a female bodybuilder in one of those muscle-head magazines).

The Army has about 15 different and very good definitions of what *discipline* is. I just happen to like this one.

Make regular and personal contact with your counterparts to your right and left. Not doing so regularly breeds an exclusionary climate and, over time, a feeling of isolation within the larger organization.

How can you have teamwork if you don't talk to your peers on a regular basis? There are times when you will not agree on things, but why complain in secrecy about it? If you have open lines of communication and personal, as well as professional, respect for each other, then almost anything can be worked out. The same holds true for one needing to talk to their immediate boss.

I have never understood why people fear talking to their boss. If you have an opinion and/or a solution to something that you feel strongly about, why keep it inside? Two sayings apply:

It's not unmanly to agree with your boss, and

"Disagreement is not Disloyalty"

As a leader, never have your entire calendar "filled."

It allows you no flexibility and it is a darn shame when a leader says something like, "I am not in control of my own schedule." You are the leader, so you better be in charge of doing those things that a) are truly important and b) are the things that only you can do.

Leading Organizations. It is not such much what
you do or how much you accomplish, but what you
do/accomplish with what you have to work with.
How high the bar (the standard) is raised is in direct
correlation to the unit's, or individual's, potential.

Could a very good high school basketball team win the Olympic Gold Medal? Doubtful. Should a conglomeration of the NBA's best? Absolutely. I think that standards of **leadership** are really based on a sliding scale. Do not be confused. This certainly does not include general standards of discipline that are all known. Everyone must meet the standard on the proper way to wear the uniform, physical fitness, etc regardless of how good, or bad, the unit is collectively. Here's my example of sliding scale standards for leadership:

A commander who takes over a terrible unit (one well below standard) and turns them into a solid, steady unit (now meeting the standard regularly) is a far better leader and a far more valuable asset to the organization than is the leader who inherited a wealth of talent and made no noticeable improvements to it. The second leader's unit may, in fact, still be better than the end result of the first leader's efforts, but I'll take the leader of the first unit over the second anytime. He made a difference and a positive one.

"Badges and resumes" impress most soldiers and
junior officers initially, and in many circles afford you

**the opportunity to at least get your foot in the door.
That honeymoon lasts about two days.**

A fairly lengthy tip for such a short summary. A leader's success is dependant on those he leads. An impressive resume means little to the soldiers unless it is matched by your actions. Their "vote on you" is cast within a New York minute. I love the infantry because it is a "No slack, no sympathy, no whining, no excuses" environment. The troops you lead decide how good you really are, not the amount of badges you have earned. This isn't the Girl Scouts.

❧❧❧

**The function of leadership is to produce more leaders,
not more followers.**

Many leaders get high marks for **what** they accomplish, sometimes regardless of how they accomplish it. In a "doing" organization like the Army that is to be somewhat expected, but that only scratches the surface of a larger, longer-term issue. Some achieve success **in spite** of others (the leader does all the work himself because he doesn't trust anyone else), or **because** of others (subordinate members carry him along), or **on the backs/by the sweat** of others (leader is so demanding and controlling that everyone does the work purely out of fear/ possible repercussions).

Leaders with a broader perspective understand that true growth of individuals and, in the long term, the success of the organization rests on the ability to create an environment where freedom of action and decision-making authority, within this climate, is done out of habit.

When subordinate leaders carry out complex tasks without your presence, or even without your input, and it is done to the leader's standards, then leadership "Nirvana" has just been achieved. Take a picture and call me if and when this ever happens because lots of factors can deter you while working toward that end state.

Strive to never be the "But Man."

You know, the kind of guy when others refer to him say things like, "He is really smart, <u>but</u> has no people skills," or "He's the most organized guy I know, <u>but</u> he treats his family like crap," or "He's the best officer I ever worked for, <u>but</u> it's a shame he's so fat that he couldn't lead from the front." You cannot be everything to everybody, but try and eliminate as many "buts" as you can.

If there is a major problem in your unit start looking for the cause by applying ever widening concentric circles around your desk.

This clearly speaks to the ownership and accountability that leaders have for their organization. Some leaders like to play the "blame game" and it typically becomes their undoing. Identify and solve problems, do not create them.

ᴖᴖᴖᴖ

"Nothing is impossible for a man who does not have to execute it."

I loved this quote the minute that I heard it. I was an operations officer at the time and was bemoaning the impact on our unit as a result of our higher HQ's latest "great idea." My battalion commander's response was the above and it rang true to me… still does.

ᴖᴖᴖᴖ

Be mindful and wary of the leader who artfully changes the use of pronouns depending on the circumstances.

The above thought comes purely from experience. When the members or smaller teams within an organization do great things it is fully understood that the leaders at echelons well above the act are equally happy with the outcome. They don't have to be "credit hogs" to feel this way; they are oftentimes truly proud of the units' achievement. "**We** did a great job on that…" "**Our** people are to be commended for their great effort…"

The really good leader maintains that collective spirit through the good and bad and shares in both. Be watchful of the leader who deftly interchanges the pronoun when things do not go well. "Why is **your** team way behind the others on this task?"… "I have seen a decline in **your** section that **you** need to apply some personal effort toward improving."

The simple math is that the higher the leader's "We/Our" threshold is before the pronoun gets changed, the better he/she is.

Be polite, be courteous, but have a plan to crush everyone you meet, just in case.

This is more about my own warped belief of life in general than it is about the Army or leading soldiers. It's not paranoia. There are lots of folks out there who have "agendas" and they aren't always about team play and the betterment of the organization. You should be friendly to all those who deserve it, but never mistake a smile and a handshake for someone who is truly your friend.

At the end of the day (meaning your career), all that will be remembered about you is: a) how you treated people and b) your reputation.

My book, my opinion. The Army has a great way of boiling careers down to an endless list of statistics but in the end I believe the legacy you leave is in those that you positively affected.

Avoid the inevitable temptation to define the quality of your service by the rank, title, and position held at the end of that service.

At some point in a career you will have risen as far as you will go. Resist the negative energy that can come with that: sadness, bitterness, missed opportunities replayed, envy, etc. Who you helped, how you served and led others, the standards you maintained, and the integrity you kept are all much better things to focus on as the end of a career comes closer.

Summary

Typically the word "summary" would imply a wrap-up of sorts on all that has been written thus far, but if you didn't get it the first time then you probably won't benefit from a summation. I will leave you with this:

All the great leaders that I have had the pleasure to serve with really understood that if they placed good **people** in the right **climate**, with a shared **purpose**, then everyone feels compelled to **contribute** above and beyond what they normally would give.

People, Purpose, Climate, Contribution.

Guthrie

www.ingramcontent.com/pod-product-compliance
Lightning Source LLC
Chambersburg PA
CBHW050354290526
45785CB00006B/2770